Cowgirls

CONTEMPORARY PORTRAITS OF THE AMERICAN WEST

Cowgirls

WITHDRAWN

Edited and photographed by

Ronnie Farley

Crown Trade Paperbacks
New York

NOTE ON THE PHOTOGRAPHS: All the photographs in this book were taken with Kodak Tri-X film using Nikon F3, Leica M4-2, or Hasselblad 500 C/M, and were printed by David Wong Custom Photo Lab of New York City.

Frontispiece: Tara Miller, Big Piney, Wyoming.

Published by Crown Trade Paperbacks, 201 East 50th Street, New York, New York 10022. Member of the Crown Publishing Group.

Random House, Inc. New York, Toronto, London, Sydney, Auckland

CROWN TRADE PAPERBACKS and colophon are trademarks of Crown Publishers, Inc.

Manufactured in the United States of America

Design by Lauren Dong

Library of Congress Cataloging-in-Publication Data
Farley, Ronnie.
  Cowgirls: contemporary portraits of the American West / Ronnie Farley.—1st ed.
  1. Cowgirls—West (U.S.)   I. Title.
  F596.F22   1995
  978'.0082—dc20   94-27701
                                                                          CIP

ISBN 0-517-88180-2

10 9 8 7 6 5 4 3 2 1

First Edition

To the women of Wyoming

and in loving memory of

Rudy Martin, Dennis Starkey, and Jake Crain

CONTENTS

Outside Farley, New Mexico.

PREFACE

My first encounter with cowgirls was in New York City, far from the sound of hoofs and the smell of sagebrush. I met a woman named Ben Formby, whose mother founded the Cowgirl Hall of Fame and Western Heritage Center in Texas. Ben fascinated me with stories about women who ran cattle and who rode broncs and bulls. Learning about the women who had made their mark on the West since the frontier days—and continue to do so today—drew me into sharing this story.

Hollywood myth and romanticism may have forgotten them, but with or without their husbands and families, women were an integral part of western history. Through every story runs a common thread of hardship, determination, and independence. It was never easy being a cowgirl, and as I learned more about their lives, I could only begin to admire their spirit.

It begins with the land—the open spaces of the West, where the forces of nature shape destiny. The livestock are at the cen-ter of a cowgirl's existence, and she must help them survive in a harsh and unpredictable environment. Only when one has to care for animals, coaxing them to live in the extreme conditions of Wyoming winters or New Mexico summers, does one begin to appreciate and understand the power of the natural world. Life on the land may be a struggle, but unlike the desperate man-made struggles of urban living, it is a struggle that fulfills and exhilarates rather than embitters and degrades.

The work is hard, very hard. Some days it truly never ends, lasting from sunrise to deep into the night. Far away from the nearest town, a winter storm can turn into a desperate race to save a herd; a sick animal can mean long nights of administering medicine; a birth among the herd transforms every cowgirl into a midwife. The care of the animals comes first. It is a care that comes from love and respect. Animals are not only a cowgirl's livelihood but also her reason and purpose. In addition to the ani-mals, the ranch itself needs care. The fences must be mended continually, the equipment needs to be maintained, and the house and barns must survive another year of exposure to the wind and the rain. For women with families, the responsibilities are even greater. Raising the children and feeding the family are still primarily a part of their work, above and beyond the duties of the ranch.

At the rodeo, one can find some of these women as they challenge a sport that has always been thought of as male. You will find no members of the weaker sex here, especially among the rough stock competitors. Taking on a ton and a half of angry snorting bulls or wildly thrashing broncs, these women are defining the sport every bit as much as their male counterparts. Rodeo cowgirls have been bitten by the lure of the road—the thrill of competition draws them from their weekly routines to travel hundreds of miles for a few seconds in the arena.

The cowgirls I met were distinct, impressive, and unforgettable. They loved what they did, where they lived, how hard they worked. They shared a strength in will, the dignity of people who overcome life's difficulties and turn them into joys. In an age of self-consuming greed, their attitude seemed to set them apart from the rest of the world. In their own right, they are a traditional people, carrying on a way of life—a way of thinking—that may be only glimpsed at today.

Ultimately, there is something inspiring about these women. Cowgirls have not taken the easy road. Yet somehow the road they have chosen for themselves has left them stronger. As I look at these photographs and remember the cowgirls I have met, all I can say is, they were really living.

Ranching Women

Tack room, Chase Ranch, Cimarron, New Mexico.

Ranching folks are hardworking people. Their days begin before sunrise and continue past sunset. During calving or lambing season, the family will take turns every two hours to check on the mothers and help with the births.

These are not big corporate ranchers, but small family operations that have been in the business for generations. The women are hardy and have strong convictions. They insist that ranching is not about money, but a way of life. It is an all-consuming, isolated world. Some expressed the drawbacks of the isolation. Others expressed fear of losing the isolation to a growing world of crime and violence.

In Big Piney, Wyoming, I was fortunate to go on a cattle drive with Tara and Mike Miller and to witness a calf birth at the Guio ranch, where Landa and Tayton Guio are an integral part of the ranch operation and help their parents in between the times they attend school. Also in Big Piney is Talli Manning, who is an outfitter with her husband and helps her sister Tara of the Miller ranch when needed. Pam Ready, who is infamous for her "pet" moose, runs half of her family's cattle business on her own. We spent an afternoon up at her "cow camp"—a temporary trailer in the woods, where she

keeps an eye on her cattle in the pastures. In Daniel, Wyoming, during a biting winter sunrise, I accompanied solo rancher Kathy Miller as she fed her livestock from a horse-drawn sleigh.

All the women I met were very friendly, open, and willing to share their lives. Eleanor Johnston of La Barge, Wyoming, spoke fondly of her great-grandparents and proudly displayed photographs of them. They were one of the first black families to come to Wyoming. Her daughter, Carrie Starkey, spoke of the importance of raising children around animals. Sheep rancher Mary Owens of Midwest, Wyoming, shared that sentiment, and her neighbor Billie Jean Beaton chatted about the old days at the stockyards. Cowgirl Hall of Famers Gretchen Sammis and Ruby Gobble have been running the Chase Ranch together for the past thirty years in Cimarron, New Mexico. Like everyone else, they wouldn't have their life any other way.

In between chores, we would sit and visit over a cup of coffee or I'd become an extra hand and work alongside them. Whether it was rounding up sheep for a shearing at Mary Owens's place or moving cattle with Tara and Mike Miller, the whole experience seemed to affect my senses profoundly because it was so new to me. In the silence of the night, I could hear the animals' voices ringing in my head; during the day, I would see their faces as cloud formations in the sky. The land itself was equally affecting. It seemed to possess a beauty that at times was pure poetry. I could understand why these women preferred being outdoors on the land and in the sunlight, despite the hardships of the elements and their work. Most women describe a feeling of a profound nature during the brief moments of calm in their hectic day: an existence of a spiritual or God-like presence out there on the land. Having experienced this firsthand, I can say only that it is a feeling that has stayed with me, and has become a recurring source of inspiration.

Road to Shamrock Ranch, Midwest, Wyoming.

My paternal grandmother was the first white child born in Lost Cabin, Wyoming, and she became the first mayor of Pinedale, Wyoming. My mom came out here from Omaha, Nebraska, right out of college to teach school, and she met my dad. They got married soon after they met. She was fascinated by cowboys. There is a lot of tradition in this country of cowboys marrying teachers, because women would only come here as schoolteachers. So many people around here had grandmothers or great-grandmothers who were schoolteachers.

TARA MILLER

Miller Ranch, Big Piney.

Tara Miller takes a break with sister Talli Manning during a cattle drive.

16

Tara, Big Piney.

My husband, Mike, and I train horses. That is something we have in common. Mike is a really good horse trainer. He doesn't even realize how good he is, but I do because I ride his horses and I ride other horses. Mike just puts so much more on a horse because he's ridden so much. He has worked like a man since he was five years old. He was shoeing horses when he was nine and riding rough stock at the same time. He was a real hard worker on the ranch, proving himself to his grandad and dad. They were all cowboy through and through. He spent a lot of time, I think, just trying to set his niche in the family of cowboys.
TARA MILLER

Mike and Tara Miller.

Tara working out with one of her cutting horses.

Moving five hundred head of cattle over ten miles of land, Big Piney, Wyoming.

When we first got married, we had a cow-camp job for nine years up in the mountains just herding the cattle. But the situation changed. I became a mother and we started to run the ranch. You're forced into a different role from the one you really wanted to do. You've got kids to raise and a ranch to take care of.

I help Mike a lot. I like to calve and save the little babies. But as far as being a cowpuncher, I get real tired of it. I got burned out up there at cow camp when I had to do so much of it. The glamour wears off after a while. Getting up at three in the morning and trailing the cows all morning, that's fine. Then the sun comes up, you get hot, the flies start biting, and your horse is tired and you're tired. It gets old. It's just plumb work, but you still like it. You go up and down all day—you get second winds. It's real wearing because you care about every little calf. Sometimes you don't feel like you got them all. You worry a lot about them because we go so far. I always worry if they're ever going to find one another. And by the end of the day, you're kind of proud of yourself.

TARA MILLER

Tara on a cattle drive outside Big Piney.

Cattle crossing, Big Piney.

My most pleasant memories are of cowboying. There are moments on those drives going up the mountains— oh, there are moments. God, it's just so beautiful, and because it's just so wonderful, I feel enlightened.

TARA MILLER

Tara at the end of the day, Big Piney.

Moonrise between Big Piney and La Barge, Wyoming.

It's real pretty out here and socially there are a lot of good things. The lack of violence and crime is nice. You don't have to be scared. It's also easy to survive in little towns—to get what you need as far as shelter and food. But living here, I sometimes feel I'm in a stagnant situation. There's only so much expanding you can do completely on your own. We have a library, but still, it's not the same as if you read something and talk about it with other people or take classes. It's just not an intellectual artistic community here at all. I wish there was more of that. I think in this day and age, in every little town, people should have access to college classes. People in real small towns end up in little ruts a lot of times. I think that's a major part of the big alcoholism problem here and everything that goes along with the alcoholism—family dysfunction, hostile feelings between people. I think more available education would help a lot. For one thing, it would give people job-advancement opportunities, something to look forward to and build on.

Talli Manning

Talli Manning, Big Piney.

An outfitter's license gives you the right to charge money to take people fishing, on pack trips, or hunting—basically recreational use of the land. Now all the ranches are turning into entertainment farms. It's nice for people to be able to experience going on a cattle drive, but it makes me sad because it gets less authentic all the time. People are having to do things like that in order to keep their standard of living. With ranching, there's not a guaranteed income. You have to keep a good nest egg or you could end up out of business. Most people are in a position where one bad year would put them out. But you never know; you could have ten bad years. There could be a ten-year drought. You have to depend a lot on the weather and things you can't foresee.

TALLI MANNING

I like to be a cowgirl; that's my favorite thing to do—move cows or chase horses, to be outdoors on the range. I like action riding, like when we gather for a branding; the horses are breaking back, and everyone's running around real fast. It's a real rush. I think that's what I like, the rush. It does have its grueling side. Some days are the most wonderful in the world, and other days, I'll ask myself, Why am I doing this?
TALLI MANNING

Above and overleaf: *Talli on a cattle drive, Big Piney.*

Talli injects antibiotics into a sick calf while Pam Ready prepares to give him medicine through a long tube.

Since I work these cattle, they get to know me and I get to know them. They get to trust you. Bud Williams in Alberta runs a seminar and uses all women in his feedlot. He said that you need to keep your mouths shut and your hands in your pockets to move the cattle. It proves to be less stressful to them. The stress level on the cattle can be very, very high, say, if you run them with motorcycles. It's just like people with stress; it really knocks the weight off. You try to handle cattle on horseback after somebody has run them on a motorcycle. It's a zoo. Those cattle are just crazy. That's why I love going on the forest where we've got our cattle, because there are no motorized vehicles up there whatsoever. It's all horse travel, period.

PAM READY

29

Pam up at cow camp, outside Big Piney.

Right now, I'm going up to cow camp every night. I take a horse and kick cattle on up and check the salt grounds and make sure everybody's doing all right, and they're all scattered. I usually come in about dusk and stay up there. The next morning, I get up, perk some coffee, and then head on down to the house to do my chores. If I need to move my cattle, I've got my dogs there. My dogs are better than having five cowboys around. They're just hard to replace. Plus, they're very protective of me, and in this day and age, you just don't know what people are going to do anymore.

PAM READY

Pam outside Big Piney.

Pam on her way to town, Big Piney.

I've been around moose long enough to know which ones I can trust and which ones I can't. Moose are known to be deadly. Boy, they can strike with their front feet. But Miss Mouse will protect me from the rest of them and she tries to run them off. You can sense which ones are your buddies. They're a lot like cattle. They've got a certain temperament. I trust my animals more than I trust most people. It would be really hard to change from ranching and cowboying and being with all the animals. If I had to have a nine-to-five job, go in and be a secretary or do something like that, it would be very hard to handle because I've been so used to handling this up here by myself. It would be rough to have to leave Fish Creek and all my moose. You might as well cut my heart out.

PAM READY

Pam at home with her moose, Fish Creek Ranch, Big Piney.

Kathy Miller loading hay on her sleigh to feed her cattle out in the pasture, Daniel, Wyoming.

All year round, I get up anywhere between five and five-thirty in the morning. Most of the time, it's a seven-day-a-week job. Of course, ranching isn't a very profitable business, even in good years. It depends on cattle prices. You sell your cattle for whatever they'll give you. For me, it's more a way of life that I like. If you're out to make money or to have a lot of money, you'd better find a different occupation.

Those cattle are like our kids. My cows are always fed before nine in the morning. I make sure they have enough hay and that they have good shelter, enough water, salt, and all the things that they need to look healthy and keep healthy. I try to be there to make sure that they don't suffer, especially during calving. Almost every cow is seen more than once a week to make sure that it isn't sick or hurt. We spend a lot of time doctoring them and running them through the chutes to vaccinate them, just like you'd do with a dog or a cat to keep them healthy.

KATHY MILLER

Kathy distributes the hay to her cattle while giving commands to her workhorses.

Kathy on her way home after feeding her cattle and horses.

I like being outdoors. I like the wide-open spaces—you can see for miles. Oh, I love it here. I don't know what else I'd do. It gets real hectic and stressful sometimes. But usually, if it gets real stressful, I can take a day off and go up in the mountains with a horse and just ride around and look at my cows. It's better than taking a two-month vacation. I don't think I could have a job where I was inside all day. I get to the point sometimes where I'd like to spend a day in the house, but one day is all I can handle!

KATHY MILLER

The Guio family:
Landa, Cynde,
Cotton, and
Tayton, Big
Piney.

In the summertime, I exercise the horses first thing in the morning, before the flies get bad. Then I have to feed the cattle. If we're calving, I'll get things ready for my dad or mom to pull the calves. Then we give cake [a mineral supplement in the form of large pellets] to the heifers. After everything is done with the feeding, we usually come in for lunch. Afterward, we go back out, and every day we have to do something like move cows or fix fences. That will take up most of the afternoon. Then I'll come back and ride my horses again. I usually ride them twice a day. And that's pretty much a full day. I like it here a lot. I'm not too sure what I want to do—what I want to major in in college. I'm thirteen now. I think eventually I'll be here ranching.

LANDA GUIO

Cotton Guio removes quills from a cow who met a porcupine.

I remember my first calf birth, because my sister and I were here. My mom and dad were out. My sister and I went and looked and one cow was calving. We called our neighbor and he said he would be up right away. We got the calf and started to pull it.

By the time our neighbor got here, we had already pulled it, and it was born. We were so proud of ourselves. We were just little and we had watched my dad do it a thousand times and helped him maybe a hundred times, but we had never done it by ourselves. So that was pretty exciting.

LANDA GUIO

Landa reaches into a cow to pull her calf while her sister, Tayton, looks on.

A calf is born at the Guio ranch.

I tell my boys, "If you have animals, you have to take care of them." At the same time, they learn responsibility. When we sell the cattle, that money will go into a savings account for them. We'll probably butcher two; then whatever money they get out of their calves is theirs. So it's nice for them. The boys don't know they're going to slaughter. They just know they're going to get some money when we sell our calves. They don't know when we butcher the pigs. They think we just get them fat and sell them. It's a mean trick to pull, but they're too little to grasp death. We had a calf die at the end of May. When he died, it was really hard for the kids. They didn't understand it, but it's something that happens all the time when you own livestock.
CARRIE STARKEY

Carrie Starkey with her son Kodi, La Barge, Wyoming.

Betty Wardell nursing a calf, La Barge.

My great-grandfather Archie Step was born a slave in Kentucky, and when Lincoln freed the slaves, Archie decided he was going to come west. He worked out here for two years and then he went back to Kentucky, and he talked about it so much that his son Lon [Alonzo] decided to come out. He came out to Wyoming and he worked on the Rathburn ranch. Then he and his father decided to homestead, so they homesteaded down on the Green River. Then they bought up some other ranches. They were pioneers in the area and everyone knew them and respected them. They were among the few black people who were educated. Back in those days, black people could barely write. Archie saw that all of his kids got to go to college. They were aware that in order to succeed, you had to have an education. My grandfather was one of the county commissioners and he was a brand inspector. They attained high status in the community, but it all stemmed from that one ex-slave who knew that you had to learn to read and write.

ELEANOR JOHNSTON

Eleanor Johnston, La Barge.

We thought of ourselves as having it very hard, but we were so fortunate because we had our own milk, our own meat, our own eggs. We grew our own garden. We grew our own oats and grain for the cows and the horses. We used to make all of our own clothes. We learned how to crochet, knit, and sew, but I loved to paint. My dad was a great musician; my mom was quite the pianist and she also played the violin. So we were taught an appreciation of music. We kept ourselves occupied and we learned to listen, because we listened to the radio. Listening to the radio encouraged you to use your imagination and you created pictures in your mind as to what was going on. You listened to other people; you learned to communicate because all you had were one another to talk to. We would have dances and picnics and Halloween parties at our house because our house was the biggest one. Everyone would bring their children—you never left your children at home. The boys would play music, and people would dance. When other people were going without, we were self-reliant. People really need to get back to thinking that way.

ELEANOR JOHNSTON

Moonrise over La Barge.

46

South Dakota.

We used to grow things without any problem, such as tomatoes and squash other than zucchini. We used to grow corn, also to feed the animals. These are things we knew we would be growing in our gardens. And you can't grow those things now without a lot of work. You might get some corn to head out, but not a lot. We always got two cuttings of alfalfa, but there again it's probably because we were able to start haying sooner, and where it was warm, it probably grew faster. Our summers used to be a lot warmer than they are now. Even fifteen years ago, it was a lot warmer than it is now. But our winters were very severe, too, so we never had a water shortage that I can remember until I was an adult. One summer, we had a real water shortage, but nothing like we have now. We don't get near the precipitation that we used to. I've noticed the change even in this little valley, and I'm going to say it's over the last maybe ten years. I think industry and man's greed have really started to destroy the earth. And we are well into destroying it.

ELEANOR JOHNSTON

47

La Barge, Wyoming.

Wyoming.

Someday if you're ever out here after a rain, look at the sky. It will be a deep, deep blue. I love the sky after a rain because it's so blue and so beautiful. I remember the blue, blue skies when I was a child. I think it's a paler blue now because of pollution. I also remember being able to see the Wind River Mountains just as clear as if they were five or ten miles away. I could also see the Uinta Mountains, and now you cannot see them down there. It's caused by all the industry down there. These mountains aren't as clear as they used to be.

ELEANOR JOHNSTON

Entrance to Shamrock Ranch, Midwest, Wyoming.

When I was in about the fourth grade, as I remember, we had the stockyards at Salt Creek. It was during the Depression and you could go down and buy colts for twenty-five cents. So I had all these horses and I would ride out and help the ranchers bring in their livestock and I'd help people work their sheep. That's the reason I got so acquainted with ranchers. I knew who would be coming in next week—I had it all mapped out in my mind. That was my life. Most little kids wouldn't try something like that when their folks are not even in the business. Finally, as I was growing up, people would ask, "Where's the good grass?" I would tell them, Well, it's out there, or over there, or someplace else. I met so many people from different counties. I even got to be friends with them. I just lived for those stockyards. And when they took them down, my world went to heck.

BILLIE JEAN BEATON

Billie Jean Beaton with Jim and Mike Owens at Shamrock Ranch.

Billie Jean at Shamrock Ranch.

The chicken coop is about three and a half to four miles in the snow out and back. I'd get a sack of corn and drag or carry it over there. I only got there about once a week, but it would last a week. Oh, once in a while I'd try and go out twice a week, but we had terrible snowstorms. Well, last winter I thought I needed exercise, and I had on these real high overshoes and the snow was real deep. Johnny would let me out at the gate and I'd say, "Okay, you drive on. I'll just walk on up." He'd get to going pretty fast up there and I was trying to run all the way up there. Usually, I was going north, into the cold. I made that trip twice or three times in one day. The next day, I was so sore. I thought, What in the world is going on with me? And I slowed down and got well. I was just trying to hurry too fast in that deep snow. But I couldn't imagine any other life really. I'm still doing the work—still haying and riding. The cooking, I hate; it's one of the vices you have to have to exist. Oh, it isn't so bad, but I'd rather be outside, even though it's tough at times.

BILLIE JEAN BEATON

53

Mary Owens of Shamrock Ranch.

I grew up just twelve miles from here. Between our ranch and my cousin's ranch, we had about 12,000 head of sheep and we ran 350 head of cattle. So I had lots of practice growing up. My three brothers, my cousin's three girls, and I were out in the corrals from the time we were little. We would spend one month docking lambs; we were the docking crew. Docking means cutting off the lambs' tails for sanitary reasons, castrating them and giving them the necessary shots for their health and well-being, and then branding them. It's done every spring. You have to handle each lamb and take it to each area where it's doctored. They're long, grueling days. Sometimes we would dock a thousand head at a time. We would start at daylight, which is usually four-thirty or five in the summertime. Then we'd be done around eight or nine in the morning. We'd go home and eat, rest for a while, and then gather sheep for the next day.

MARY OWENS

54

Bill and Mary Owens separate their sheep for shearing according to coarseness or fineness of wool.

Mary with her son Mike.

The winters will take part of what you've got no matter how hard you work. It's a tough, hard life, but the rewards are good. I can't imagine raising children anywhere else. And we're so close to each other. Sometimes being a twenty-four-hour wife is not all it's cracked up to be. It's hard, because anytime you have to work so close for twenty-four hours, you get a little testy. But you're both working for the same thing—betterment of your place and care of your livestock, and what one doesn't see, the other one will. If there's an animal that's sick, maybe one will see it, but the other one won't. Between the two of you, you get something accomplished. We're running all the livestock totally by ourselves. It's a lot, but we know what's going on, and we're out there all the time—going through the hills and seeing how things are. It's worth it if you enjoy it. You really have to like it, because it's tough and very physical. It's nothing to have to handle seventy-pound bales of hay. It's just what you have to do.

MARY OWENS

56

*Mike and Bill
Owens.*

Our own children were six months old when we were taking them on horseback. By the time Jim was a year and a half old, he was riding eight hours with us in the front of the saddle. This is typical. You have your children there with you. You have no one to take care of them, so they're with you no matter what you're doing. Sheep are wonderful because they won't hurt the children. You can set them right beside the corral while you're working the sheep. You take your kids with you because you don't have an alternative and it's a real healthy environment.
MARY OWENS

Sheepshearers at Shamrock Ranch.

Agriculture is so important to us all because we're all consumers of agricultural products. Anything that we eat and most of what we wear is from agriculture. If we don't understand about agriculture, then we can't make good, sound decisions, and our government will dictate things that they don't have a clue about. We need to educate our youth about it. I work with young people and try to educate them about agriculture. Less than 2 percent of our population produces the food for the country. Every rancher and farmer here produces enough food for thirty-six people, and that's a lot.

MARY OWENS

Shorn sheep, Shamrock Ranch.

As in any business, there are abusive people. But those people don't survive. If we don't take care of our land, then it's gone next year. That's the only thing that feeds our livestock, which is the only thing that feeds us. We have no choice but to take care of it if we plan to stay here. It's instilled in us. You have to like what you're doing, because economically you get by, but you don't make a lot of money. The rewards are when you walk over the hill and you're walking with your sheep, you really know that God is right there, and that's about as religious as most ranchers are.
MARY OWENS

Wool being collected and bagged.

Moving sheep out to pasture.

Gretchen Sammis at the Chase Ranch, Cimarron, New Mexico.

Gretchen photographing repairs needed on her truck.

I don't know whether you can call it a spiritual thing, but you do have those feelings. Actually, we are just stewards of the land, and God put it here. It's definitely our obligation to take care of the land and to nurture it and not abuse it. If we don't take care of the land, we're shooting ourselves in the foot. If land is not used properly, then it could become overgrazed. One thing is to conserve it and use it wisely. Nature will always gets its way—everything balances—but when Mother Nature gets mad, she's going to cream us, so that's it.

GRETCHEN SAMMIS

Gretchen with her dog up at the cow cabin.

Gretchen checking on her horses.

Cows are different. Some cows are the nicest cows to do anything with and others are real bitchy. In the wintertime, when we have them down here and we are out feeding them every day, you get to know them like you do people. They all look different. Some are sweet and they'll come right up and eat "cake" out of your hand, while some of them just stand off and never want you to get close to them. They appreciate your feeding them, but not to the point where they would come right up to you.

RUBY GOBBLE

A few of the cattle at Chase Ranch.

Ruby Gobble, Chase Ranch, Cimarron, New Mexico.

Ruby's whittling.

We worked hard for thirty years trying to develop what we think is a pretty nice cow herd by going and buying good bulls, and better bulls, and keeping what we thought were our better heifers to go into the herd. Our friends tell us it's a really nice cow herd, so we are proud of it. You really have to work at it. You always have to keep on top of it. Our life is hard work, but I never get tired of it.
RUBY GOBBLE

We're working and dealing with men all the time. Most of the guys are very supportive. Some of them are going to say things to us no matter what; they're just that type of person. But the majority of them aren't like that. Years ago, the pioneer women got out and worked in the fields with the men and went back in the house because they had to cook the meals and take care of the family. The old saying is, A man's work is from sun to sun; a woman's work is never done.

RUBY GOBBLE

Ruby picking vegetables.

People need to be educated. People in the inner cities need to come in contact with living things. They don't see the sky or feel dirt. It makes a lot of difference. The farmers are only 1$\frac{1}{2}$ percent of the population now. We have a lot of people in suburbs and a lot of people who are weekend farmers, and we have a lot of people who live in the inner cities. We have to get to them all. It's education and sitting down and talking. We are supporting their lifestyle, their good food. Sure, some food is imported, but the majority of it comes from here.

GRETCHEN SAMMIS

68

The cow cabin at Chase Ranch.

To some people, going to church is the most important thing in the world. That's fine if that's how they get their satisfaction, but it's not for me. I don't feel like you have to go sit in a church to get close to God. You can go out here and sit up on your own rock and you can feel His presence. You look at the land that has been providing for you. We do everything we can to try to protect the land and try to make things even a little better if it's possible.

Land is definitely how we make our living. A lot of times, I just ride and get up here in the mountains. I never get tired of enjoying the beauty of it. Being here thirty years and riding all over, there are times I'll see something that's a little different, something I never noticed before.

RUBY GOBBLE

"Ladies' Steer Undecorating," Bill Pickett Invitational Black Rodeo, Denver.

Rodeo Gals

Rough-stock gear,
Amarillo, Texas.

The rodeo life is a subculture unto itself. The sport of rodeo was invented by cowhands who decided to test their skill against one another during slow times on the ranch. Uniquely American, it has grown into a national sport of international fame. In some areas, it is the only form of entertainment to be had, and hundreds of people come from near and far to compete or watch.

I began with the Women's Professional Rodeo Circuit. The women who compete must travel frequently, often leaving home or work on a Friday night to drive through several states for a few seconds of competition. In most rodeos, women compete only in barrel racing and sometimes calf roping, but in the women's rodeos, there is also the rough-stock competition—bronc and bull riding. The women's rough-stock riding was something I wanted to see.

Bull riding is considered one of the most dangerous of all sports. It requires a high degree of mental discipline. A rodeo bull weighs about sixteen hundred pounds and is quite lively for its size. The cowgirl's score is based upon how tough the bull is to ride (each bull is handicapped by difficulty, and cowgirls draw straws for which bull they will ride) and how skilled the cowgirl is in staying on. In order to qualify for a score, the cowgirl must stay on the bull for six seconds. But staying on is only half the sport. Once the cowgirl is off the bull, she must get out of the arena; otherwise the bull will come after her. She must be fully alert, even if injured, for hesitation could cost a cowgirl her life. With the assistance of the rodeo clowns and bullfighters, who taunt the bull into attacking them instead, the cowgirl must quickly get to safety. Rodeo clowns and bullfighters not only entertain the spectators but also protect the cowgirl from danger.

Bareback bronc riding also has a six-second requirement, but a bronc will not try and kill the cowgirl afterward. The bronc is also handicapped by difficulty and straws are drawn among the competitors, but in addition to staying on, the cowgirl must come out of the chute spurring the horse in order to qualify for a score.

Highlighting the rough-stock competition of the Women's Professional Rodeo Circuit is a grandmother named Jan Youren, who comes from Crouch, Idaho. She has eight children and fifteen grandchildren. She is a world-champion bronc rider and a 1993 Cowgirl Hall of Fame Honoree. She grew up breaking horses and has been participating in rodeos since she was twelve.

Other strong contenders are Tammy George, who has world-champion titles in both bronc and bull riding and is the

Bull rider Tonya Butts, Professional Women's Rodeo Finals, Guthrie, Oklahoma.

owner and stylist of a hair salon in Brentwood, California; world-champion bronc rider Vickie Crawford, who works in the oil fields in Wyoming and Idaho; and bronc and bull rider Candy Bell, who works for the Gila River Indian Reservation.

In addition to the Women's Professional Rodeo Circuit, there's the black rodeo circuit and the Indian rodeos. At the Bill Pickett Invitational Black Rodeo in Denver, I felt a great sense of pride and dignity from the participants as well as the spectators. The traditional cowboy's prayer that is recited at every rodeo seemed much more emotional. The announcer said the prayer and dedicated it to the children, "especially those who grow up before their time." At that particular rodeo, there was a boy being honored—a survivor of a drive-by shooting. He was given a standing ovation as he was led around the arena on horseback. The people there were very warm and friendly.

That is where I met barrel racers Marilyn LeBlanc and Carolyn Carter. Winning at barrel racing requires the fastest execution of a cloverleaf pattern around three barrels spaced in a triangle across the arena. Marilyn is the champ at this sport and the top money winner of the Bill Pickett Invitational Black Rodeo circuit. Carolyn is a registered nurse in Oklahoma City and also works for the Bill Pickett rodeo circuit.

Unique in this particular rodeo is "Ladies' Steer Undecorating"—where the contender, on horseback, pursues a steer and attempts to remove a ribbon from his shoulder—and "Co-Ed Ribbon Roping"—where a cowboy will rope a steer while at the same time the cowgirl must run from the chute where the steer was released, grab the ribbon off the roped steer's rump, and run back to the chute for a timed score.

The Indian rodeo at Rosebud, South Dakota, was part of the annual Rosebud Pow-Wow, where one could hear the traditional powwow songs being performed in the background. The rodeo announcer spoke in Lakota as well as English, and women competed in barrel racing and calf roping. At Pine Ridge, the neighboring reservation, I spoke to Jonnie Clifford and Leslie Johnson, who both gave up barrel racing to start families but shared pleasant memories of the sport and rodeo days.

In all the rodeos, I felt a deep sense of family among the participants. There was a strong connection that crossed all lines. It is a connection that combines the cowgirl life with the draw of the road and the anticipation of what new experiences lie ahead.

Jan Youren with her husband, Jim, their son Cole (left), and her grandson Zane, Crouch, Idaho.

76

My dad broke a lot of horses when we were young. That's more or less how he made a living. If anybody wanted a horse for a kid, Daddy would take the rough off of him, and then I got him. I made lots of kid horses. So I had ridden lots of bucking horses—it was natural. Daddy gave me a horse when I was six. She was just a yearling. He said, "You can have her, babe, if you can break her." I didn't have a saddle, and oh, this little rip. I'd ride her and she'd buck me off, and when you got bucked off, you got back on. That was the deal. Then there was one day she probably bucked me off five or six times. I was out of sight of the house; nobody could see me. She bucked me off. It was a dirt road, but a hard road. I didn't want to get back on her and I threw rocks at her. I did everything to try to get her to run home so I wouldn't have to get back on her. But she wouldn't do it. I had to get back on her anyhow. She had me ride her clear up to the house and bucked me off again. So you know, through that kind of thing, I was used to riding bucking horses.

JAN YOUREN

Jan fastens on her chaps at the Professional Women's Rodeo finals, Guthrie, Oklahoma.

When I was twelve years old, Daddy produced one of the very first all-girl rodeos they ever had in Idaho, and he entered me in every event. I won fifty-four dollars and I thought this was the road to riches, man! Twelve years old and fifty-four dollars for twenty-four seconds' work— how can you beat that? This is my thirty-eighth year in rodeo and I'm still on the road, so it's been a fairly long season.
JAN YOUREN

Jan checking her taped shoulder, Guthrie.

Oh, I've got a lot of war wounds. One time, I was riding in Phoenix, Arizona, and the horse threw me back into the announcer's stand and I hurt my back. So I went to the doctor and he x-rayed it. The impact had actually pulled my ribs away from my backbone. He said, "Boy, you're lucky you didn't hit down where you broke your back." I didn't know what he meant, so I looked at him kind of funny and he said, "You've had a broken back." I said, "Not that I know of," and he said, "Lady, you've had a broken back and it's not very long ago. Come look at these X rays." It had been broken way down. None of the other doctors had ever found it.

Jan Youren

Jan getting ready for her ride, Guthrie.

Jan on a bronc, Santa Fe Stampede Pro Women's Rodeo.

Above: *Jan being awarded a saddle by her fellow competitors for her 1993 induction into the Cowgirl Hall of Fame.*
Right: *Jan receives a congratulatory kiss from her husband, Jim.*

The cowboys don't like it real well. Although at the Cow Palace in San Francisco (I didn't make it the first year; I had ribs broken in the back), Bruce Ford and some of these other big-name cowboys said these girls should be home barefoot and pregnant in the kitchen, not out here pumping it up against a rigging. And by the time that rodeo was done, Bruce Ford (and I'm proud of the boy) came forth and said, "The girls that I came here with today, I leave feeling the utmost respect for." He said, "These girls are athletes, and they have a place."

JAN YOUREN

The bruises are tough to get rid of after riding all weekend. Monday morning, getting out of bed, you're a little sore. It's not like when you're eighteen or nineteen years old. As you get older, it really does become tougher. I don't see how Jan Youren does it. She's one of the toughest ladies I know, if not *the* toughest. You've got to give her credit.

TAMMY GEORGE

Jan's first try at her new saddle.

Vickie Crawford on site at an oil-rig operation in southeast Idaho.

My jobs have always been nontraditional. I've always worked almost exclusively with men—blue-collar construction stuff. The way to get by there is to be kind of like one of the guys but not quite. You don't chew and cuss. It's individual, I guess. My female friends are the ones who are at rodeos. Even if they're five states away and we just run into each other at the rodeos, it's good to have that friendship. It's carried on for fifteen years. There're a lot of women who have quit to start their families and come back because they miss it and they missed their friends. This is their club.

VICKIE CRAWFORD

When you go to a rodeo, it is similar to a family reunion. You see people you know and catch up on what they've been doing, whether it's been a month or a year since you've seen them. There are some real good competitors. Some women are more standoffish, but in my mind, that's their space. That is one thing that I've noticed: People give you your space, especially in the rough-stock competition. If you seem to be really focused on something, they're not going to come up and ask you what you did the night before. Yet even if it's unspoken, there is the nod of the head or a "Good luck." You know they want you to do well and they want to do well themselves. You get upset if you haven't done well yourself, but if someone else does real well, you can always appreciate a good ride.

CANDY BELL

Rough stock competitors share stories, Amarillo, Texas.

Calf ropers, Santa Fe.

Women are competitive in different ways than men. There's a lot of jealousy and envy among us. The only thing that keeps us from being nasty and wicked to one another is that there're so few of us, we can't turn against one another. It's kind of a blessing that way.
VICKIE CRAWFORD

Calf ropers visit in between competitions, Santa Fe.

Calf roper, Santa Fe (both pages).

I started barrel racing and did a little bit of goat tying and team roping. My brother rode bulls and bareback horses. When I saw him and his friends having so much fun at the rodeo, I'd go behind the chutes right after I'd get done running barrels. Being behind the chutes with the guys, the whole atmosphere was different from running barrels. It just looked like a lot more fun. So he took me under his wing and he and a couple of his friends taught me how to ride. I started riding steers, then I practiced riding bulls and started riding bareback horses, and I gradually quit running barrels. So that's where I've found the most happiness in rodeo.

TAMMY GEORGE

Tammy George taping her bronc rigging, Professional Women's Rodeo finals, Guthrie, Oklahoma.

Tammy climbing onto a bronc, Professional Women's Rodeo finals, Guthrie.

People don't know that there are women out there who ride bareback horses and bulls. When they find out that I ride, they just don't think I fit that image. What they have in their mind of a bull rider or a bronc rider is a rough-tough tobacco-chewing cowgirl. And I don't think that I'm any one of those. A lot of the girls I traveled with when I first joined the Professional Women's Rodeo circuit don't fit that image, either. They had long fingernails, wore makeup, and had their little earrings in. They're not rough-tough girls. When I have to be, I think I'm tough, but I don't think that you have to have this look about you to do what we do.

TAMMY GEORGE

I can honestly say I've never been afraid to sit on the back of a bareback horse or a bull. I've always said whenever you are afraid, it's time to hang it up, because that's when you're going to get hurt. You have to be real positive and totally focused on what you're doing. If you're out there and afraid of what you're doing, how can you have fun at it? It's supposed to be fun.

TAMMY GEORGE

Tammy on a bronc, Santa Fe.

Cindy Baker leans back and gives the nod of her head for the gate to open, Professional Women's Rodeo finals, Guthrie.

Faith Taylor and a bronc are released from the chute, Douglas, Wyoming.

Vickie Crawford on a bronc, Professional Women's Rodeo finals, Guthrie.

While on a bronc, I'm not real aware of sounds. And I don't see much. I'm just feeling more than hearing or seeing. You can ride them without even being in sync with them at all. And you can spur them decently without being "tapped out" [in sync]. But when you're tapped out, it's beautiful. And time warps on you. The first few broncs you get on, you don't have time to be cognizant of anything or react to anything. Everything comes by you in such a rush or a blur. Time passes really fast. But the more you get on them, it seems like you have time to make minor adjustments, think about what's happening, change something, wait a little bit or hurry up. It's probably like when people have car wrecks; they say everything was in slow motion. I don't know if that's the effect of adrenaline. It's a dangerous situation—getting on a bareback horse or a bull. I think people innately crave that danger element. It's part of being human.

VICKIE CRAWFORD

Bull rider Donna Shelly receives an adjustment by a chiropractor before her bull ride, Professional Women's Rodeo finals, Guthrie.

think anything related to sports is more mental than physical. Sure, you have to be a little strong and you have to be a little bit balanced, but so much of it is mental. You can practice and get on bulls and horses, but you can also practice in your mind. Just try to visualize yourself doing everything right—from chute procedure to doing a perfect ride, right down to hearing the buzzer and jumping off. You try to visualize matching moves for moves with the bull. That's what goes through my mind. I think you also have to be very positive. I know what I'm capable of every time I get ready to ride. Part of that is the mental attitude—staying positive. Some people might think I'm a little cocky, and maybe I am. You have to be a little bit cocky. You've got to know how to be a winner. You have to know you're better than that bull or that horse and you're going to ride him tonight. I know every time I nod my head for that gate to open, I'm a winner. I am very sure of myself. That's what gives me an edge. If I am bucked off, oh well, I learned something. I know why I was bucked off and I'm going to fix it. And if I buck off the next time, it's not because I made the same mistake twice.

TAMMY GEORGE

Tammy George on a bull, Professional Women's Rodeo finals, Guthrie.

Candy Bell is taped by her friend Jodi, Professional Women's Rodeo finals, Guthrie.

The biggest thing in rough-stock competition is the fall—being able to tuck and roll. If you fall flat, you're just going to get hurt and you make a bigger target for something to hit. If you can tuck and roll and keep moving, then you're not a stationary target. . . .

My dad was a bareback bronc rider. But when he and my mom got married, she said no more riding. You can get injured pretty badly and I guess she was thinking in the long run of whether or not he'd be able to have a job and support the family. So he quit riding. He was real excited when I started riding broncs. It's kind of neat because it is a bond that my father and I have. I love it.

It's a whole different ride on bulls than it is on broncs. Because on a bronc, once you get off, you just make sure that he's not going to run over you. But on a bull, there's always the potential that he could turn back on you and come after you. The ride is not over on a bull until you or the bull is out of the arena. It's a different type of rush. There's a little bit more adrenaline. I know that I can get hurt, but I'm not afraid getting up on the animal. I don't have fear. I've got respect.

CANDY BELL

Candy before her bull ride, Professional Women's Rodeo finals, Guthrie.

Cowgirl and bull are released from the chute, Professional Women's Rodeo finals, Guthrie.

104

Cindy Baker on a bull, Professional Women's Rodeo finals, Guthrie.

 lot of people say, "Oh, you went out there and you beat that bull." In my mind, it's not beating the animal; it's being able to get in sync with it for that amount of time—being able to feel the motion and be in the same rhythm.
CANDY BELL

Bull rider, Santa Fe.

It makes the difference if the bullfighters are good. Some people say if the bullfighter doesn't like you, then he's not going to help you. I haven't seen it happen, but I know it's happened a couple of times in the men's rodeos. The bullfighters made a halfhearted attempt. I'm not sure why they would do such a thing. It could be that previously the person may have put them in danger when they shouldn't have, or they weren't watching out for themselves, or they may have said something. Sometimes I wonder if they're teaching that person a lesson. Like hey, you've got to watch out for yourself—I'm not the Almighty Savior out here. It's to teach them to respect the animals a little bit more, because some people get out there and once the buzzer goes off, they think that everything's done—and on a bull, it's not.

CANDY BELL

Bull, Denver.

People tell me I'm crazy. They say, "You could be killed on a bull." And I say, "Yeah, I can be killed in a car accident." With the world as it is, you could walk outside your home and be shot in a drive-by shooting, too. There're all kinds of possibilities. But my philosophy is, I'd rather be doing something that I enjoy than being paranoid about leaving my home. And it's fun; it's a lot of fun.

CANDY BELL

Tammy George and rodeo clown–bullfighter, Professional Women's Rodeo finals, Guthrie.

I had an old boyfriend who said, "That's not very feminine, is it?" And I said, "Define *feminine*!" The only definition I can come up with is the behavior displayed by the female. The same is true with *masculine.* I thought that was really an odd thing for him to say, because he's raising his two daughters all by himself—nurturing and caring for them. Isn't that considered feminine behavior?

VICKIE CRAWFORD

Vickie Crawford being interviewed by champion bull rider Don Gay for TNN.

Vickie and her roping horse, Rock Springs, Wyoming.

It's only a part-time sport for women, which is probably best, because you can't quite get taken away from real life. Have a balanced life and don't ever make it first. I've seen people who had a lot to lose because they put their priorities on a temporary thrill like rodeo. Whereas if you keep your long-term goals in mind and make it part of your short-range plan and put as much into it as you can, you'll do well. Because I've found that rodeo is the only thing in life that pays you back 100 percent for your efforts. Working for somebody else won't do that. Rodeoing will.

VICKIE CRAWFORD

Pine Ridge Reservation, South Dakota.

When I was little, I just followed my grampa around all the time. He more or less took care of me. He was a horseman, so I was used to being around horses. I was the little tomboy and I'd help him haul bales of hay and cut wood. A lot of kids used to ride horses then, but now you don't see that very much. We had all these little Shetland ponies in different sizes and we used to ride them around in gangs in Pine Ridge. Back then, all the kids rode horses; now they're into riding motorcycles and driving cars. It's really changed.

JONNIE CLIFFORD

Jonnie Clifford and her horse, Pine Ridge Reservation.

I remember when I was barrel racing, we used to haul my horse in the back of the pickup with one of the tall racks on. That's how I used to get my horse around to the rodeos, because we didn't have a horse trailer. It was easy for him to get in when we were at home because we had a place that we backed up to and he walked into the pickup. But when we got to the rodeos, we'd have to find a little hillside or something. Half the time, we couldn't find one, so he'd end up practically jumping out of the pickup!

JONNIE CLIFFORD

Barrel racer, Rosebud Indian Rodeo.

Leslie and Josie Johnson, Pine Ridge Reservation.

We were around horses when we were little kids. Whenever I wanted to compete, my parents helped me; they were real supportive of me. Once you get started in rodeo and you like it, the urge will never die. You're hooked. I'm sure Josie will grow up around it and she'll probably carry it on, because that's how I got started. If she doesn't want to, that's fine. It's just when you grow up around it, you more or less get it in your blood, too.

LESLIE JOHNSON

I think Indian rodeos are starting to be more familiar to people. I travel with my husband a lot in the pro rodeo circuit. A lot more Indians are getting involved in the pro rodeos than ever before. The rodeo people get along with one another. It's more like family because everybody has the same interest in common. They all communicate pretty good. For most of the people in the professional circuit, that is their living, because they have no time for anything else.

LESLIE JOHNSON

Colorado.

Some people just get into rodeo and they think because they buy a horse, he's supposed to go out there and do everything right. And that's not the way it goes. You've got to work hard for things to come out. Everything you do nowadays is going to cost you some money. You've got to buy a truck, a trailer, and you need a place for your horse to stay. There're 365 days in a year, so you're going to have to feed him every day and you're going to have to give him hay. Then if you rope, you have to buy some cows or some cattle to rope. Anything you want to do, you've got to work hard at it.
MARILYN LEBLANC

Horse trailer, Bill Pickett Invitational Black Rodeo, Denver.

Rodeo contestant with baby, Bill Pickett Invitational Black Rodeo, Denver.

I started as a little girl. I was a tomboy. My dad rodeoed, and I always went with him. If we went to a roping, we stayed half the night. It was just me and him. Now when I go to rodeos, he calls and says, "How did you do this weekend?" And I tell him. He's real supportive. You've got to have somebody in your corner, even if you mess up. You've got to have somebody say, "Oh, it will get better." Years ago, when he rodeoed, they didn't have that many black people in rodeos. He said back then they did not give blacks recognition for what they had done. Black people did not really participate. They kind of held them back. So now, he's glad to see them come on out and participate.

MARILYN LEBLANC

Marilyn LeBlanc, Bill Pickett Invitational Black Rodeo, Denver.

120

Denise Henderson in "Co-Ed Ribbon Roping," Bill Pickett Invitational Black Rodeo, Denver (both pages).

When we first started going to rodeos, everyone would ask, "You ride horses?" But people are not surprised anymore. This started out as being the only black rodeo association, but now there are three associations, and they keep us going just about all year round. This way, we get to travel and the whole family gets involved and it keeps us busy.

CAROLYN CARTER

Carolyn Carter with her daughter Tiffanie, Bill Pickett Invitational Black Rodeo, Denver.

Carolyn Carter on her barrel horse, Bill Pickett Invitational Black Rodeo, Denver.

You just can't come to a rodeo and borrow a barrel horse, because you won't know what buttons to push on that horse. In barrel racing, 90 percent of the win is your horse. He's the one that has to take you around the pattern, and if you're used to him and you know him and you know what buttons to push when you get to a certain spot, you should go home with a check. Having your own horse is the best way to do it. It takes a lot of work, but you're a team.

CAROLYN CARTER

Santa Fe.

Animals

Pine Ridge Reservation, South Dakota.

nimals are at the core of a cowgirl's life. Whether she is a rancher or a rodeo competitor, she respects the animals of her world.

For the rancher, her primary function is taking care of the animals, for they are her livelihood as well as way of life. She is constantly checking on them, feeding them, tending to the sick, and helping in the birth of the newborn. The extreme forces of nature—snowstorms, subzero weather, and drought—dictate her world. The rancher must see the animals through weather changes and other natural phenomena, and do so in a way that minimizes the stress and discomfort on them. She develops a sixth sense about them as if they were her own children.

All of the animals provide an important function on the ranch. The horses, cows, and sheep are the sustenance. Dogs round up cattle and sheep by nipping at their heels to keep them together, and cats keep down the rodent population. Each is an important component in the whole, and those who don't carry their own weight eventually get the boot.

In the hierarchical order of animals on a ranch, horses are at the top, and there is a bond between horse and cowgirl that is unparalleled. Horses and ranchers must work together to round up animals, check the fences, and survey the land. To horse lovers Tara Miller and Carrie Starkey, it is the most unique and heartfelt of relationships.

Cattle have distinct personalities and routines, yet they are fragile animals and need constant care. There is a sense of curiosity about them, and they behave very much like humans. In addition to cattle, sheep are the economic mainstay of some ranches. Sheep are kid-friendly but need constant surveillance. They often fall prey to coyotes and must be constantly protected by both rancher and trained dogs.

A rodeo gal is a team with her animal. Whether it be a six-second ride on a bull or a bronc, or a race around barrels on her horse against the clock, the animal's performance is part of her score. An important part of the sport is her sense of understanding and respect for the animal—knowing what it is capable of and not abusing that knowledge.

Carrie Starkey with her horse, La Barge, Wyoming.

130

It's like a love affair with animals. I've had my horse that I rope on longer than I've had my husband and my little kids.
CARRIE STARKEY

You've got to be able to figure out when your horse isn't feeling good or if there's something wrong with him. You can't just ride them; you've got to take them to the vet. A lot of people get horses and just turn them out. They just get all they can out of them and just boot them out in the cold. They don't go check on them, and then they die. If you take care of them, they're going to take care of you and they're going to give you all they can give you until they can't give you any more. To me, they're kind of human, too. They want a bath, they want to be dried off, they want to roll, and they want their backs scratched, too. And my horses get all of that. My husband tells me I spoil them, but I want them to realize that they're something special.
MARILYN LEBLANC

When you get to know a horse pretty good, you know his ways and he knows yours and he becomes your friend. Some people and animals don't match up. A lot of people get mad and beat their horses. But a horse remembers things. I had a horse one time that just hated men because a guy beat him all the time. Every time my father or any of my brothers got too close to him, he would know it; he could sense it. Even when I had a man shoe him, he had to be tranquilized, because he would just kick at the guy.
LESLIE JOHNSON

Tara Miller tending to her horse's leg, Big Piney, Wyoming.

I think every horse has a purpose in life. I just have such deep respect and love for them. Ever since I was little, if I ever had any problems, I'd go talk to my horses. I was a real late bloomer as far as being interested in boys. Looking back, I know it's liking horses so much that kept my mind off boys. I think it's really good for little girls to have that opportunity rather than being upset over teenage problems. Once in a while, if I feel bad, I still go down and just put my arms around a horse and smell him and feel him, and it gives me strength. They are such a noble, wonderful animal.
TARA MILLER

Kodi Starkey and a pinto colt, La Barge, Wyoming.

My son Kodi's horse, Tom, is a godsend. When we bought Tom, he was only for Kodi. Kodi started riding and showing him. It has really changed Kodi a lot. It's built up a lot of personal confidence for him. Kodi's not nearly as shy, and he's not afraid to go any-place on his horse. He takes care of his horse. He feeds him and brushes him, and we have to bathe him. It's all work and he's good about it. He's real good about making sure Tom gets his medicine, too. After they won their trophy and their ribbons, Tom put his head down and Kodi just squeezed his head. It's a good life for kids.

CARRIE STARKEY

Mother Goose with Aleeshia, Chris, and Mark Denison, La Barge.

Mother Goose, the hairy pony, is thirty-two years old—and that is ancient for a horse. They start going downhill at about eighteen. We have spent more money in medication to keep him alive, because the kids won't let us put him to sleep. In reality, that would be the kind thing to do for him. But he's a pet, and how do you say good-bye to your pet? They all love him and he loves them.

CARRIE STARKEY

Carrie and Jared Starkey, La Barge.

People think cows are stupid, but they're not. Every one of them has a personality. They're outsmarting you and they're not going to do what you want them to do. Range cattle even have baby-sitters. They get about four or five calves and one cow will stay there with them. And the rest of them will go graze or go to water and then come back. But there will always be one cow right there with them. They're also very regimented. When they eat, the same cows will follow the feed wagon forever and the others will stop and eat. Everyone has their own niche.

GRETCHEN SAMMIS

A mother cow with her newborn, Miller Ranch, Big Piney.

There are some people at the rodeos who are real cruel to animals, just as there are some people in the medical field who are real sadists and there are schoolteachers who are really mean to kids. People like that exist. You can't attack and shut down the entire cattle industry because of those people. Some of the worst things that I have seen happen to horses are done by people who have no intention of being mean to them, but they just don't understand them. They don't know how to ride and so they end up putting sores on the horses' backs. Most people in the cattle industry love their animals. They wouldn't be in that industry if they didn't love their animals. People here judge other people by how well they take care of their animals. It's a matter of respect or disrespect.
TALLI MANNING

We leave the bulls out for sixty-three days because a cow will cycle every eighteen to twenty-one days. So a cow has three chances to get bred. Before we ship, we put all the cows in the orchard and we run them all through the chute and pregnancy-test them. So we'll ship the cows that are not carrying calves, unless we know the reason why, because there's no point in feeding a dry cow.
GRETCHEN SAMMIS

A cattle drive, Big Piney, Wyoming.

Fish Creek Ranch, Big Piney.

We have to use computers a great deal in our work just to keep up to date as far as what cows are doing. We have a history on cows and how many calves they have produced, and if they can't produce a certain amount, then they're gone. We can't afford a cow who can't pull her own weight.

MARY OWENS

Cattle truck, Guthrie, Oklahoma.

Mary Owens tends to a sick lamb, Shamrock Ranch, Midwest, Wyoming.

Shamrock Ranch.

The night the storm hit, we were still lambing. I told Bill, "It's raining," and that's the worst thing. Sheep will survive a cold snow, because it's dry. But the snow mixed with rain—that's what killed them. By four o'clock, it was his shift. He said, "There's about five inches of snow." By nine o'clock, there was fourteen inches of snow. We were out there from seven in the morning until two-thirty the next morning nonstop. There was snow up to my waist and the wind was blowing at forty-five miles per hour. We tried to get them off the fence line. We tore the fence down, but we couldn't move them because of the wind. The sheep were getting covered up. We built a hut for the ones that we did get. During all of this, we had our two little children with us. They stuck with us all day. We came in for lunch—I was just so exhausted and the little boys had to eat. We were gone for forty-five minutes and when we went back, there were fifty dead sheep. It just tears your heart out inside to stand there and be so damned helpless. It's like a nightmare. You see them lying there, even in your mind. It's tough. Anytime those horrible things happen, it's emotionally devastating. Economically, it's horrible, but that's not the big thing. It's what it does to you inside. Mike had a corn feeder, so he and Bill loaded up what they could. And these were sheep that were within three months of lambing. So these sheep weighed 170 pounds each. The two of them lifted eighty head of sheep up into the corn feeder, and they could bring in only eighty at a time. They brought them in and I'd go down and medicate the ones that looked really rough. Then the ones we built the hut for, they got hypothermia. It was pretty tough—you're stronger after it's over, but it takes a long time. It proves you try your very hardest to take care of them no matter what, because that's your job. The next day, it was perfectly clear, as if nothing had happened. Any rancher has experienced something like this sometime, because that's just how nature works.

MARY OWENS

It takes a lot of years to really learn about animals and how to handle them. You have to learn to work with them and get them to want to be with you and just give you their all. If they don't like you, you know it.
PAM READY

Miller Ranch, Big Piney, Wyoming.

La Barge, Wyoming.

Mike Owens with friend, Shamrock Ranch.

In the winter, the horses will come and swarm around the hay, and the kids just think it's wonderful. They will be standing on the hay, handing out handfuls and treats and pats. It's really funny. Here it is a raging blizzard, and the kids are riding in the back of the truck, having fun. It's good because they have to be nice so the animals will come to them and respect them and be nice to them. No matter what, as soon as we pull up—whether it's feeding time or we're just checking on them—they're happy to see us. It's an unconditional love. That's good for Kodi and Jared. They have to be responsible at an early age. Even in the dead of winter, they have to be responsible. Maybe I started them too young, but it's a good life for them to show kindness and respect. And then they get it in return. It's a good thing. I hope I'm doing right by them.
CARRIE STARKEY

Carrie, Jared, and Kodi Starkey, La Barge.

Tesa Manning with her dad, Miller Ranch, Big Piney, Wyoming.

Children

Jim and Mike Owens, Shamrock Ranch, Midwest, Wyoming.

148

On a ranch, baby-sitters are rarely used, so the children are outside on the land with their parents when they are very young. Growing up in a ranching family means chores and responsibilities because the welfare of the animals takes precedence. It is a life surrounded by animals in the great outdoors. It is a life that revolves around the family as a unit working together for the same goal. Everyone, no matter what age, has to contribute. Their lives are shaped by the animals and elemental forces.

Children being children do find time to play, and on a ranch there are a million things to explore. Jim and Mike Owens play while Mom and Dad sort the sheep. Jim is four, already has his own horse, and can ride by himself. Mike is two and a half.

Kodi and Jared Starkey of La Barge, Wyoming, both have horses and share the responsibilities of taking care of them and the cattle. As their mother, Carrie, explains, it is important to teach them responsibility. In addition, it increases their self-esteem.

Tesa Manning of Big Piney, Wyoming, is too young at the moment to ride by herself, but she does get to ride with her dad leading her. She also helps her mom in cooking and in the chores of her parents' outfitting business.

Although they are still isolated, some ranch mothers worry that the family ranching way of life is eroding with each new generation, as corporate ranching takes over and better opportunities in the outside world lure children away from the family business. Others worry more that escalating crime and violence in the outside world will affect their children's futures. Each mother hoped that she had instilled in her children the strength to succeed and survive in an uncertain world.

Cowgirl with baby, Santa Fe.

A lady from Chicago was saying, "Oh, it would be so wonderful to raise kids here because there is no crack." And I said, "Yeah, but there is such a high rate of alcoholism, and that can be just as devastating." The problems become so deeply embedded and then increase with each generation unless someone is strong enough to turn it around before they pass it on to their kids. On the other hand, a lot of the ranch families have real strong family structures. The children know their grandparents and spend time with them, and there is a family network where each person has something they can contribute to the children.
TALLI MANNING

Tesa Manning at home, Big Piney, Wyoming.

Hanging out in the arena before the start of the Rosebud Indian Rodeo, South Dakota.

If they don't get to ride, they're mad.

CARRIE STARKEY

*Kodi and Jared Starkey,
La Barge, Wyoming.*

If they're not interested in horses and rodeo, I don't have a lot for them to do. Those that are, I can keep busy. Those that aren't, I can just see them getting further and further into alcohol and stuff. You've got to give them a little independence and a little trust. I don't sit on my kids all the time. They also know if they don't do it right, I'm going to come down pretty hard on them. But they know they're trusted and that if they go wrong, they're going to have to pay for it. Kids are their own best police.

JAN YOUREN

Jan Youren with her son Cole, Professional Women's Rodeo finals, Guthrie, Oklahoma.

154

Boy being honored at the Bill Pickett Invitational Black Rodeo, Denver.

Boy with his horse outside Pueblo, Colorado.

156

We expect them to do things young. They have livestock of their own and they learn to take care of them. Because that's how everybody's brought up on a ranch. That means if it's ten-thirty at night and you come in and you're tired, that horse is taken care of before you, or if it's dead hot in the summertime, those animals have to be watered before your needs are met. And that means going out through terrible blizzards to protect what you can, because that's just what you do—that's your job. So hopefully we instill that in our children.

MARY OWENS

Texas.

ACKNOWLEDGMENTS

To the women and families highlighted in this book I extend my sincere thanks for taking me in, sharing their lives, and in some cases putting me to work in the midst of their daily life.

To my partner Alex Ewen, thanks for his constant support, encouragement, and friendship. To my parents, Rita and Jack Farley, and my family, my continued gratitude for their support. To my agent Stephany Evans, thanks for her belief, stamina, and sense of humor. To my editor Peter Ginna, thanks for the extra effort he has extended over the years on behalf of my work. Special thanks to Miriam and Judith Gideon for their considerable support, to David Wong Custom Photo Lab, The Solidarity Foundation; Zoë Yanakis, Jeffrey Wollock; Jane Feldman, Holly Cara Price, Donna Daniels, Axel Kessler, Suzanne Hanlon, Helene Silver and Lily Malcom, James Turk, Philip Shaw, Fernando Natalici, David Joseph, Erika Stone, Will Lewis, Ben Formby, SIR Studios; Michael Johnson, Mel Terpos, J.P. Reali, Chuck Orozco, Ben Newberry, and Tom Good. To Margaret Formby and the Cowgirl Hall of Fame and Western Heritage Center; Pam Minick, Billy Bob's and the Fort Worth Stockyards; the Lazy E Arena, Guthrie, Oklahoma; Rock Springs, Wyoming, Chamber of Commerce; Cindy Gruell, Olivia Harrison, Lydia at the WPRA office; Charles Boozer of the Bill Pickett Rodeo Circuit; Lani Hunt, Kelly Mull, Vic McDarmott, Marie and Misty McDarmott; Kay Meeks; and B.J. Griffith.

Heartfelt thanks to all the families and friends who made me feel at home on the road: Doyle, Carol, and Heather Keeton; Marilyn and Walt Pourier, Lori Pourier and Bently Spang; Ingrid Washinawatok-El Issa; John Trudell, Quiltman, and the Grafittiman Band; and Isabel and David Martinez of Las Vegas, New Mexico.

Marilyn LeBlanc, Bill Pickett Invitational Black Rodeo, Denver.